A WALK AROUND
THE CASTLE OF CHILLON

Claire Huguenin
With the collaboration of Anna Pedrucci

Translation: Dr. Cecilia Griener Hurley

**FONDATION DU
CHÂTEAU DE CHILLON**
Avenue de Chillon 21
CH-1820 Veytaux
Tél.: +41 (0)21 966 89 10
Fax: +41 (0)21 966 89 12
Email: info@chillon.ch
www.chillon.ch

Editorial Deborah Lockwood and Marta dos Santos | Fondation du Château de Chillon
Translation Dr. Cecilia Griener Hurley, Neuchâtel
Graphic designer BONTRON & CO, Genève
Printer IRL SA, Renens

ISBN 978-2-8399-0397-4

NTENTS

text is based on research carried out for the new museographical presentation by Bernard Andenmatten,
iotech SA (Anna Pedrucci), Atelier Saint-Dismas (Eric-J. Favre-Bulle and Alain Besse), Flavio Cazzaro, Danielle Chap-
  Adrien Guignard, Claire Huguenin, Francesca Nussio, Eva Pibiri, Brigitte Pradervand, and with the generous sup-
of Catherine Kulling and Daniel de Raemy.
ation du Château de Chillon, 2008.

3

North and west sides of the castle.
*(Fondation du Château de Chillon.
Photo Elise Heuberger)*

OME HISTORICAL FACTS

e areas are indicated by letters in brackets referring to the names of parts of the castle (see plan, 3 cover). These are then followed by numbers indicating different points of interest on the tour.

fording the only negotiable route between the steep mountain and the lake, the site s been occupied since the end of the Bronze Age, as can be seen from some of the man remains excavated from tombs near the castle. There is no evidence of human tivity on the rock itself, despite the discovery of a bronze bracelet in one of the lower- el rooms of the present building (P); this clearly ended up here because it was thrown along with earth used for backfill.

natural moat separates the limestone rock from the banks of the lake; on the other e, there is a sheer drop into Lake Geneva. It lies alongside the route leading to the eat Saint Bernard Pass, one which has been exploited since Antiquity. This rather usual and special position must have meant that a fortified building was constructed re fairly early to watch the traffic. Nonetheless, no archaeological evidence has come ight to prove that there was any presence here before the 11th century, that is, after supposed Roman camp which has long been believed to have existed here. No real torical facts are available to indicate the name of the proprietors. From the High Mid- Ages, the Chablais – whose name derives from *caput lacus*, indicating the lands at end of the lake – came under the abbey of Saint-Maurice d'Agaune. It seems that House of Savoy already exerted an important degree of influence over this religious tre during the 11th century, and that by the middle of the 12th century it was firmly lanted in the area.

Bronze bracelet, 10th-9th centuries BC.
The oldest object found in the castle, discovered in a lower-level room. It comes from a tomb and was thrown away in earth used for backfill coming from the castle or its immediate surroundings.
(MCAH Lausanne. Photo Fibbi-Aeppli)

5

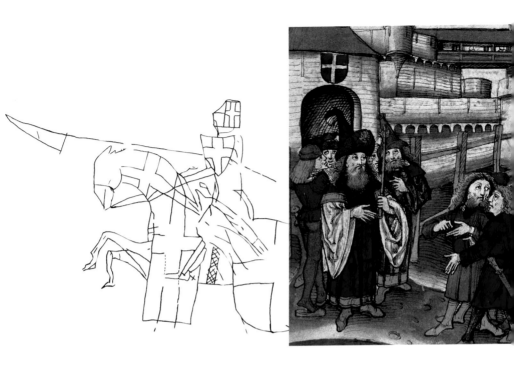

The Savoyard Period

Explicit reference to the castle is first made in 1150, when it is said that the Counts Savoy controlled it, having acquired the rights to it, or sharing them with the sires Blonay. As a result, they also controlled the route along the shores of the lake. In t document, Chillon is referred to as a *castrum*: given the mediaeval meaning of the wo this proves that there was a settlement associated with it.

During the 13th century, the Counts of Savoy conquered most of the territory of Va divided as it was into a number of small seigneuries. This marked the beginning of Sav domination over approximately two-thirds of the territory which makes up toda French-speaking Switzerland. The land which they had conquered lay both to the no and to the south of the Alps, and they controlled the two major routes across the we ern Alps, namely the Mont Cenis Pass and the Great Saint Bernard Pass. These tw passes, major trade routes which connect Italy with north-western Europe, proved be a useful source of income. The upkeep of the roads and the protection offered to tr ellers were offset by the taxes levied on the goods transported across the territo Because of its position on the second route, the castle was interesting for both econo and strategic reasons. In 1214, Thomas I of Savoy founded the town of Villeneuve, t kilometres above the bourg of Chillon, on a site which was large enough for the c struction of a tollbooth, warehouses for the storage of goods and port facilities.

Important reconstruction and enlargement works were carried out on the castle stages, initiated by Count Thomas I of Savoy (1189-1233) and his four sons, includ Pierre II, the master of the castle from 1255 to 1268. Pierre Mainier, a cleric from Cha

The Savoy court on its travels:
Yolande of Savoy captured by
Charles le Téméraire's men.
From Diebold Schilling, Amtliche
Chronik, III, f° 801, late 15th century.
(Bibliothèque de la Bourgeoisie de
Berne, Mss.h.h.I.3)

y, supervised the works for Pierre II. At the time of Philippe of Savoy, the brother of
d successor to Pierre, the works were entrusted to Jacques de Saint-Georges, a mas-
mason and engineer, and thus an architect who was specialized in military instal-
.ons.

e Savoy family used the castle as an occasional residence, whilst the permanent res-
nt was the castellan bailiff. Since they governed extensive territories, the Savoy fam-
needed to move from one place to another constantly in order to maintain a close
ationship with their subjects. This nomadic lifestyle was also tied in with the rhythm
the seasons, as some residences could not be used during the winter months, whilst
ers lent themselves to certain activities, such as hunting. The count travelled sump-
usly. He was accompanied by his close circle and by an entourage made up of ser-
ts and administrators. He also took with him the equipment and furniture which
uld be needed to transform the places where he stayed; his rooms in each residence
re empty and left closed when he was absent. But someone needed to be at Chillon
oughout the year, and this task fell to the castellan, usually a member of the Savo-
d aristocracy. The castellan guarded the fortress, dispensed justice and levied the cus-
ns duties and the seigneury's income. The duchy of Savoy was broken up into sev-
l bailliages during the second half of the 13th century, and at this time the castellan
Chillon took on the duties of the bailiff of Chablais. The result was that this became
 largest dominion in the Savoyard lands, covering as it did the castellanies between
ey and Aigle, in the Lower Valais, and on the south banks of Lake Geneva (Evian,
onon). The castle became a very important administrative and financial centre in
 northern Savoyard lands. Two specific buildings were therefore constructed on the

7

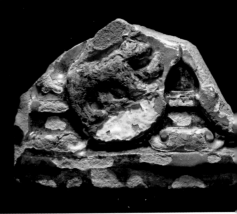

northern sector of the rock, in the area reserved for the Count. These were the *dom.*
clericorum (G), used for administrative duties, and the treasury building (K), which h
two functions. It was here that the archives were stored. However, the same buildi
was also used to safeguard currency, money which came from the seigneury and fr
the tollhouse at Villeneuve; this money was not usually sent to the Treasury in Cha
bery but was kept at the castle to be used for military operations or works.

Stained glass bearing the coat of arms of Amédée VII of Savoy and of his wife Bonne de Berry.
Copy of a late 14th-century original deposited in the Musée historique de Lausanne; copy made in 1931 for Chillon by Guignard and Schmit.
(MCAH Lausanne. Photo Fibbi-Aeppli)

At the end of the 14th century, administrative affairs were centralized and operatic
were transferred to Chambery. The court preferred to stay in other residences, such
Le Bourget, Thonon or Ripaille. In 1436, before his election as Pope Felix V, the Du
Amédée VIII tried to inject some new life into the castle. He sent his master of wor
Aymonet Corniaux, a carpenter whose duties were to maintain the buildings in Chabl
and the Vaud region. Corniaux carried out important works in the castle, and modifi
the defences at the top of the towers and the walls. However, this was not to be cc
tinued, and Chillon was destined to remain neglected until the Bernese arrived.

Fragment of a tile bearing the coat of arms of Bern,
2nd half 16th century, found in the moat in 1902.
(MCAH Lausanne. Photo Fibbi-Aeppli)

The Bernese period

The conquest of the Pays de Vaud was completed on March 29 1536, the day when t
castle of Chillon fell. The building, which had been spared by the wars of Burgundy, w
a little run down but structurally sound when it passed into the hands of the Berne
The castle became the administrative centre for the bailliage of Vevey and the pern
nent residence of the bailiff, a member of the Bernese patriciate. He bore the title of ca
tain of Chillon and, because he represented the monarch, was obliged to carry ou
number of functions.

The former division of the castle into two sectors, one for the lord and the other giv
over to the intendance was no longer necessary, and the new occupants reorganiz
the space to suit their needs; the defensive system was adapted to allow the use
firearms. In 1733, the bailiffs left this isolated and uncomfortable dwelling and mov
to Vevey. The castle was no longer seen as necessary for military operations and v

d above all for storage. In 1785, the idea of turning the northern part into an enor-
us wheat granary was mooted, but this was soon abandoned, possibly because of
impracticability of the idea and also because the area is rather damp.

e beginnings of the cantonal period

January 1798, patriots from Vevey and Montreux occupied the castle and met with
resistance. The castle became national property during the Vaud revolution and
s transferred to the new canton of Vaud in 1803. To begin with, no attempts were
de to renovate the old building; a caretaker and two police guards looked after it
d no new function was found for it. It was used to stock gunpowder, munitions and
apons for which no other depot had been found, and also to guard prisoners. The
nantic Movement rediscovered the Middle Ages with considerable enthusiasm,
d a new image of Chillon began to become popular. In his *La nouvelle Héloïse*, pub-
ed in 1762, Rousseau had already drawn attention to the site, setting one of the
sodes of his novel at the castle and alluding briefly to the imprisonment of Boni-
d. However, it was Lord Byron who was to invest Chillon with a mythical dimen-
n, when in 1816, whilst on a pilgrimage to the places described by Rousseau, he
ite his famous poem *The prisoner of Chillon*. This account magnifies the sufferings
François Bonivard (1493-1570), prior of Saint-Victor in Geneva, who was held cap-
e in Chillon because of his opposition to the Savoyards and was subsequently lib-
ted by the Bernese. The historical figure becomes a symbol of liberty and his prison
nvested with a sacred dimension. Both the castle and the landscape, against which
owers, are imbued with the characteristics beloved of Romantic aesthetics: a pic-
esque silhouette, ancient walls which bear witness to a sombre past and a sub-
e framing element in the shape of the mountains. Writers, painters and visitors
re equally enthralled by this. Yet the Vaud government was little impressed by this
vly found celebrity: in 1836-38, they altered the building so that it would be bet-
suited to the storage of war weapons, and then to new prisons. Despite this, ever-
reasing numbers of visitors came to Chillon, even though they could only visit the
tle's rooms under the watchful eye of the police guards, who also had to impro-

**Pierre-Samuel Joyeux and
Friedrich George Wexelberg, Le
château de Chillon. En allant de
Villeneuve à Vevey,**
late 18th century, coloured etch-
ing. View showing an episode from
La nouvelle Héloïse.
*(Fondation du Château de Chillon.
Photo Elise Heuberger)*

Prison du château de Chillon,
lithography after a Hieronymus
Hess's painting, 1st half 19th century. A romantic vision of Bonivard
and his gaoler.
*(Zentralbibliothek Zurich,
Graphische Sammlung)*

Balthasar Anton Dunker, The capture of the Castle of Chillon in 1798, etching.
(Musée historique de Berne. Photo Yvonne Hurni)

vise as guides until, some time later, more official guides were employed. To impr
their listeners, these guides would embellish the accounts given by the writers
poets with their own versions of romances and dramas; several of the names still u
for the rooms today are derived from these stories.

Excavations in the first courtyard (D), 1897.
(ACV, N 2. Photo Rémy Gindroz, Archéotech SA)

Albert Naef and Otto Schmid: the castle becomes a historical monument

It was during the second half of the 19th century that a different understanding
monuments began to develop. Chillon was to be one of the first buildings to be
fit from the attention that was now paid to historic constructions. The building v
judged unsuitable for modern needs, and it was decided that it should be stripp
of its practical functions and rehabilitated as a unique witness to regional hist
Johann Rudolf Rahn (1841-1912), an art historian, penned a first text in which t
scientific and historical approach becomes evident. The time was ripe for proje
related to the conservation of the patrimony, and the Association for the restora
of the castle of Chillon, allying patriotic and educational intentions, was foun
in 1887 with two main objectives, one administrative and the other financial. C
of the Association's first acts was the creation, in 1889, of a technical commiss
responsible for planning and carrying out the work necessary for saving the ca
and the area immediately surrounding it. Amongst the members of this commiss
were a number of people known for their work in the domain, such as Rahn, m
tioned above, and especially Henri de Geymüller (1839-1909), an architect, engin
and architectural historian, who drew up an entirely innovatory plan. According
De Geymüller, any restoration work needed to draw upon archaeological and d
umentary evidence and should be limited in its scale, conservative, consistent

10

The castle seen from the south,
taken by the Bisson brothers,
famous Parisian photographers,
2nd half 19th century.
*(Zentralbibliothek Zurich,
Graphische Sammlung)*

Members of the technical commission, August 5 1898, in courtyard F. Albert Naef is seated, Otto Schmid stands in the window opening.
(ACV, N2. Photo Rémy Gindroz, Archéotech SA)

should aim at a valorisation of the current state of the building, taking into acco
all elements of its historical development. Work began in 1896, under the direct
of Albert Naef (1862-1936), an architect and archaeologist who was to be appoi
to the newly created post of archaeologist for the canton in 1899. Naef was assis
by the architect Otto Schmid (1873-1957). Five years of systematic excavations
which research carried out in the archives should also be added, began to sh
results: the castle, stripped down, yielded the first secrets of its history. Howe
the desire to know and to understand everything before undertaking any work sc
met with a considerable number of difficulties. Some of the rooms urgently nee
to be reinforced; others had to be restored as soon as possible in order to show so
concrete results to a public who scarcely appreciated the implications of such lc
investigations. The room called the room of Justice (now the *aula magna*, U1.26) v
already presented in 1899, displaying its mediaeval splendour. This presentati
hailed as a model, earned the site an international reputation, and it was describ
– and was to be for a long time – as a "model of restoration". The renovation n
well have been exemplary, but it was based on a deliberate choice, that of favc
ing the mediaeval period, and included a number of reconstructions in pla
where the original structure had degraded to such an extent that mere restorat
was not possible. Naef, who never concealed his fascination for the Savoyard per
and especially for the 13th century, tended to interpret the remains from this p
of view. After the death of De Geymüller in 1909 this trend continued. The tec
cal commission did not meet again until 1927, and the overall plan for the restc
tion, which was meant to ensure a coherent approach to the works, only appea
in part. In 1935 Naef retired, and Schmid took over. The last major reconstructi

Avril 1903
Lundi, le 20

Journal des travaux, des fouilles,
trouvailles accidentelles, incidents,... etc et de l'exploration
archéologique du château,
April 20 1903, f° 1026.
The Journal was begun in 1896
and was a record of what hap-
pened each day in the castle. It
was intended as a historical record
of the work and also to ensure its
seriousness. It was to be continued
until 1976.
(ACV, N2. Photo Rémy Gindroz,
Archéotech SA)

that of the *domus clericorum*, was completed during the 1950s and Schmid th brought to an end the programme that had started 60 years earlier.

Despite the plan which had been agreed upon to begin with, almost all of the post-me aeval modifications to the castle were in fact removed. There are only three rooms wh today bear any traces of the Bernese period (B.2, S.16 & U1.18), apart from some pain decorations and military installations which have been kept. One or two utilitarian ac tions, which have proved difficult to remove, remind us of the cantonal period. In g eral the rooms have been put back into what is felt to be their primitive state, tha mediaeval, which has sometimes implied major reconstructions; many bays and f places have been recreated according to often tenuous archaeological evidence, us fragments found on the site.

The wish to display all the archaeological elements found can sometimes resul creations which are heavy and incongruous. Naef stated optimistically that . *stones speak, and that one only has to ask questions of them and they reply imme ately*, but some of the modes of presentation can arouse a certain feeling of p plexity. Openings dating from different periods are to be found one next to the ot doors appear at the top of walls; this creates a series of assembled architectural ments which are difficult to understand and whose pedagogical use and legibility need to be proved.

A similar impression of collage is given by the way in which the mural painti were treated by Ernest Correvon (1873-1965), an artist and one of Naef's prefer collaborators. The Savoyard decorations were revealed when later coats of wh

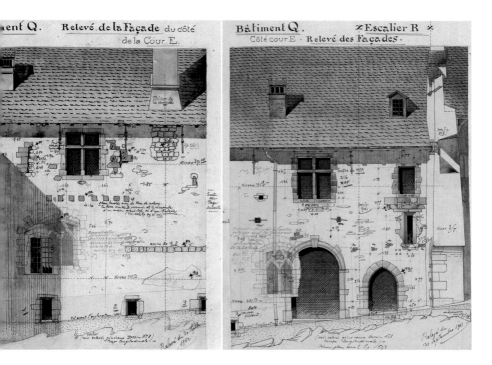

Relevé de la Façade du côté de la Cour E.

Bâtiment Q. Côté cour E · Relevé des Façades ·

✳Escalier R ✳

Otto Schmid, Drawing of Q and R on the side of courtyard E, 30 September 1902. The results of the archaeological study and propositions for reconstitutions are indicated in red.
Included in the Journal, f° 905g and 906 g.
(ACV, N2. Photo Rémy Gindroz, Archéotech SA)

sh were removed; this did not damage the Bernese decorations, and so the two now be seen together.

nts of fancy may well have gradually taken the place of the original scientific ambitions, it cannot be denied that this lengthy enterprise is fascinating and also representative only of a certain vision of the Middle Ages but also of earlier generations' attitudes ards restoration. The works on the castle have ensured its reputation and have also forced its role as a historic monument.

rk of this kind never really finishes entirely in a building of this size, even if it is true ay that the departure of Otto Schmid marked the end of a chapter in the history of lon. Work on the structure of the castle is always necessary, and this is presently usted to a group of archaeologists and restorers who apply the methods and the the- s of our age. Since 2002, the castle's running and restoration have been placed under control of the Foundation for the Castle of Chillon. This work had previously – since 7 – been carried out by the Association which now supports the Foundation's k, and is responsible for activities on the site in particular.

E MEDIAEVAL SITE AND LATER ALTERATIONS – A CHRONOLOGY

castle as it is today is the result of a series of additions around a central keep (I), *magna turris* (or Great Tower) found in mediaeval texts, which was undoubtedly structed during the 11th century and occupied a central defensive position. It otected by an almost oval enclosure, which is in turn reinforced by a glacis covering

Donjon (I), south façade.
(Fondation du Château de Chillon.
Photo Elise Heuberger)

the rock at the foot of the wall; this was intended to impede attempts either to cl
the wall or to sap it. The castle's original layout gives us some idea of the appe
ance of the site. A conduit from latrines is to be found to the north, thus proba
in an area which was not inhabited. Its main door opens towards the south, p
ably in the direction of annex buildings built – possibly in wood – in the area of
entrance now in use. Here was also to be found a stone chapel, of which only
crypt remains today. Its exact date of construction is not known, and it was inten
as the place of worship for the seigneur and for the settlement's population. It v
during the 12th century that the Tower of Allinges (X) was added, some distanc
the north of the donjon, to provide residential quarters. The layout of the site v
now determined, and it was thus in the area around this first group of seigneu
buildings that those used by the Savoy family would later be built. This was
fortress's general form, as mentioned in the document dating from 1150.
chronological order of the various buildings is certain, but there are doubts c
cerning the exact date of each of the elements mentioned here; this is large
result of the fact that the archaeological digs were carried out many decades a
Some authors tend to reduce the timescale, claiming that all the buildings were c
structed in the period extending from the end of the 11th century to the mid 1
century. Others, however, feel that the works should be dated over a longer pe
of time. An outer enclosure was constructed during the second half of the 12th c
tury, below the first one, where the gradient of the glacis changed. The south
most point of the rock and the western area did not remain unbuilt. Naef produ
some hypotheses on this question, but this is not the place to discuss them. G
erally, they have been filled in and levelled off, and only rare traces of these arch

16

General view of the castle, taken from Chillon Wood.
(Fondation du Château de Chillon. Photo Elise Heuberger)

cal antecedents can be seen; they have not been subjected to a recent criti-
eading. They have been incorporated into or given up their place for new
ings, such as the mid 13th-century watchtower (B), which is today unrecog-
le, and the large main buildings (Q & U) constructed from the mid 13th cen-
onwards on the side of the rock looking out over the lake. Other buildings were
d around the first central construction on the northern side of the rock: the
el (Y) built at the end of the 12th century, the three semicircular towers con-
ted to protect the second enclosure around 1230 (C, Z1 & Z), the *domus cleri-*
n (G) and the treasury building (K) erected during the second half of the 13th
ury. In terms of its occupation of the territory and its general appearance the
e was almost complete at the end of the 13th century, even if some new build-
were added later. These were the main building (W) adjoining the Tower
inges added during the 14th century, the entrance building (A) and the modi-
ions to the watchtower (B) at the end of the 15th century. In terms of its ele-
n, however, the castle was only to acquire its definitive silhouette during the
century; this is because storeys were added and the defensive structures rein-
d at various times.

alterations which occurred at the time of the Bernese and later, when the build-
assed into the hands of the canton, were mainly removed during the 20th century,
ng few traces of their existence. There are nonetheless some exceptions to this:
16th-century stables in the entrance courtyard (N-N1), a staircase (O) and some
ior decoration. These were commissioned by the bailiff Hans Wilhelm von Müli-
who wished to repair the damage caused to the southern part of the castle

General view, lakeside.
*(Fondation du Château de Chillon.
Photo Elise Heuberger)*

by the earthquake in 1584. The defences still show clearly, however, the alterati
made so that firearms could be used. Many key-shaped loopholes are still to
seen in the enclosures, the towers and the walls surrounding the principal co
yard. These were pierced in earlier architectural elements such as battleme
mediaeval windows or arrow-slits during the 15th century, especially in the 1
century and also later. They alternated with small rectangular openings, which w
used for keeping watch.

A BIRD'S-EYE VIEW

Chillon is the largest castle on the former Savoyard territories, 100 metres long (ab
330 feet) and 50 metres wide (about 165 feet). It is constructed on an oblong r
explaining the shape of the castle.

Chillon's double identity – fortress and residence – is clearly seen in its layout. The la
ward side is constructed for defence. On the other side, overlooking the lake, are
residential areas, protected by the lake and by the fleet, which was stationed at
leneuve. The residential spaces are divided into two parts, separated by walls and co
yards. The upper spaces, opposite the entrance, were those reserved for use by
prince and his court, who lived at Chillon only on a temporary basis. The lower spa
around the two first courtyards, were those used by the bailiff-castellan and the s
who lived there all year long. Each of these two sets of residential complexes is in
divided between private and public areas, organized in various two-storey main bu
ings. These quarters, which are also to be found in the other Savoyard castles,

The aula magna (U1) at the time when it was opened to the public, 10 June 1899.
In the background the stalls from Lausanne Cathedral can be seen.
(ACV, N 2. Photo Rémy Gindroz, Archéotech SA)

…es which are characteristic of their functions or of a range of functions. Thus the …, a vast official and ceremonial room, was used for various activities relating to gov-…ment: audiences were held here, justice was dispensed and it was also in this room … festivities and sumptuous banquets took place. At Chillon both the seigneur and … castellan each had two large rooms available for them (Q & U1). In the prince's quar-…, these rooms give onto withdrawing rooms, i.e., a space (which was deliberately …ed close to the latrines) which was sometimes used as a bathroom, or more gen-…ly as a servants' room, dressing room or small salon (U2). The private apartments …e made up of smaller rooms, called *camera*, such as the famous *camera domini*, the …gneur's room. The castellan's quarters, on the other hand, were not as carefully …mited, and seem to have occupied several different quarters.

… former service quarters, the kitchens, the annexes and the buildings used by the …vants can no longer be identified today; in some cases it is even impossible to know …ere they were situated. One exception to this is the large cellars in which goods which …ded to be kept fresh were stored (P & Q). The castellan placed the various goods here …ich were given by his subjects in payment and which, when the court was not in res-…nce, were immediately sold on or for which a monetary equivalent was demanded.

painted decorations

…llon is one of the buildings in the region, which has the most important and richest …ection of painted decors, dating from the end of the 13th century and the first half …he 14th century. They were painted in distemper and show imitation masonry …k, whose appearance varies from one room to another. The patterns differ;

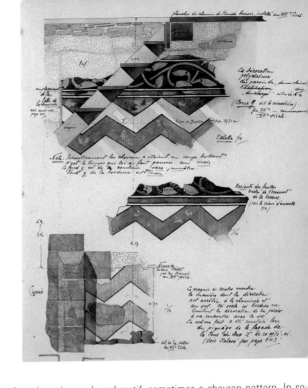

Drawing of the paintings in the domus clericorum (G), September 1900, taken from the Journal, f⁰ 671. *(ACV, N2. Photo Rémy Gindroz, Archéotech SA)*

sometimes there is a chequerboard motif, sometimes a chevron pattern. In so places, there are horizontal bands of two alternating colours, separated by single double lines representing jointing. All of these patterns personalize the individ rooms, whilst at the same time lending their walls a uniform and regular surface. main colours used were ochre red, green, black and white. Sometimes a fri made up of stylized vegetation motifs is added along the top of the walls. A spe range of motifs was used to decorate and highlight doors and windows. The ceili whether original or reconstructed, barrel-vaulted (Q.14 & U.17) or with joists (U2 & G.31), also had their part to play in the creation of this symphony of colours. hoods above chimneys, like the one in the *camera domini*, were decorated w heraldic or figurative motifs, a further contribution to the colour scheme. One of results of the work carried out during the 20th century was to impose a slightly rep itive scheme, although in some window recesses effects of greater subtlety are to be seen. This type of decoration appeared in the region around 1300, and fr 1330, it began to become more common and more complex in its effects. Naef wis to date them to 1256-65, but it is now felt that they are later, probably having be created at the earliest at the end of the 13th century. Even given this later date, t are nonetheless precocious examples of this style.

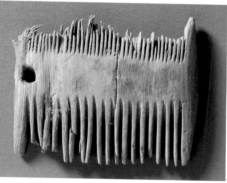

Archaeological dig in the moat,
March 1903.
Included in the Journal, f⁰ 997g.
(ACV, N2. Photo Rémy Gindroz,
Archéotech SA)

Small wooden late mediaeval
comb, found in the ditch in 1903.
(MCAH Lausanne. Photo Fibbi-Aeppli)

ROM ONE COURTYARD TO THE NEXT

e commentaries offer a tour from one courtyard to the next, with a visit to the lower-level rooms. In
neral, the text follows the route the visitor takes around the castle; on occasions, however, this order
s been modified so that all the rooms in one building can be discussed together. The areas are indi-
ed by letters (see plan, p. 3 cover) followed by numbers referring to particular features.

e first courtyard (D)

cess to the castle, separated as it is from the banks of the lake by a moat, is
ssible by means of a covered bridge dating from the mid 18th century with a
all lodge, which used to be a guardhouse. During the 19th century, the moat
s filled in and became overgrown with vegetation. It was then cleared out and
cavated in 1902-03, yielding many objects which had been thrown into this vast
en-air dump over the course of the centuries and which proved to be valuable
tnesses to daily life from the Middle Ages to much more recent times. Clearing
t the moat thus proved to be a useful exercise in terms of the information that
uld be gleaned from it, but it also meant that the rock became an island once
re, as it had been in the past. At the end of the bridge, between two towers
& C), is the late 15th-century **gatehouse** (A.1 & 38). Its outer door is protected
openings made for the purpose, visible above the bridge's roof, and by a loop-
e, which bears the date of 1589, at the height of a man. Inside the courtyard,
earlier door has been replaced by a large opening in a segmental arch, closed
a grill in wrought iron. All the entrances in this style, which are to be found at
ch point of passage from one courtyard to another, were made at the time when

the castle was turned into an arsenal; they were enlarged in 1836-38 to allow t movement of cannons. In the upper storey of this building (A.38) is the mechanis of a clock made in 1543 for the neighbouring tower (B) by the master clockmak André de Morges.

The **first courtyard** (D.3) allowed access to the castle's outbuildings and a large tow (B). Originally smaller, this space was occupied especially by a chapel which was ass ciated with the primitive castrum and by the building housing the second entran which was replaced by a staircase (O). The plan of this chapel can still be seen in o line, revealed by the presence of a different form of paving. All that remains of t chapel, dedicated to Saint Pantaleon, is the **crypt** (D.10), uncovered during the ex vations in 1897. This building must have dated from the 11th century, as is suggest by the fragments in bone or ivory from a reliquary found buried in its altar. It was lo considered to be Carolingian, but is now universally accepted to date from the 11th-1 centuries. When the watchtower (B) was built towards 1250, the chapel was abandon – it was doubtless the new chapel (Y) that was used hereafter – and then transform into storerooms before being demolished. The crypt was simply covered over and th survived underground.

The main function of the **watchtower** (B.2 & 39), which has had many names, is t of controlling the entrance. The tower as seen today has undergone many modifi tions that hide the first construction, built in the middle of the 13th century, w another storey added circa 1280. Powerful angled buttresses were placed around tower during the 14th century, forming arcades on the walls. Toward 1485 a furt

rey was added, the tower was topped off with a new machicolation and the ades were filled in. In order to show the tower's earlier form, its southern wall was tially stripped of its later additions during the 20th century. This heavy mediaeval nitecture is decorated by some more recent features, such as the 16th-century clock e, on the side overlooking the mountain; this was renovated in 1776, at which time coat of arms of Berne was added to it. On the side giving onto the courtyard is an blazoned stone bearing the date 1586 and commemorating the bailiff Von Mülinen, ponsible for the organization of many important works in this part of the castle. At top of the façade is an old sundial, of unknown origin, which since being placed e in 1951 has wisely observed that *Sic vita fugit* (So does life fly).

room on the ground floor (B.2) was turned into a guardroom in 1898-99, a reminder ne of this space's earlier uses, and one that is certainly attested in 1751. The decor s chosen accordingly, composed of a number of Bernese motifs taken from other ts of the castle (S.16, U1.18 & X.19), graffiti and sketches seen in various places. se features have since disappeared, apart from one fragmentary silhouette of a hal- dier executed in red chalk. The painted coats of arms of Berne and of Von Mülinen the chimneypiece are, however, compilations. The tower's upper storeys house a f apartment, in a modern addition outside the walls with a corridor leading to it 9). Here is to be seen the clock which, in 1897, replaced the old and worn-out mech- sm from the 16th century.

the south side of the courtyard are two former stables and cowsheds built in 1536 1586-87 (N-N1) respectively. These utilitarian buildings, which are today used

Depot (Q) looking towards the staircase.
(Fondation du Château de Chillon. Photo Elise Heuberger)

for the visitors' reception area (N.4), were altered over the centuries to suit var
functional requirements, as is evident from their rather heteroclite appeara
before they were restored at the beginning of the 20th century. At that time, it
decided to accentuate the Bernese character of these buildings: a roof with ea
and projecting dormer-windows was added, lending a picturesque style to the b
ing that was very much appreciated during that period. The height of the roofs
also dropped in order to free the end of the covered way (N-N1.40). The covered
and the bartizan, in the southeast corner, were rebuilt in 1585, after the earthqu
on a layout dating from circa 1430. They both contain important testimonies to a f
of painted decor which was widespread during the Bernese period. It may wel
in a poor state of repair, but it nevertheless bears witness to a practice, already
rent during the Middle Ages, which modified the architectural appearance of
buildings. The façades were protected by light-coloured coats of plaster an
places the underlying structure was emphasized by the application of painted
tation masonry work. This effect can be seen on part of the wall (C.37 & A.38), wh
near the entry it is white, and also in the staircase (O) in the second courtyard.

Interlude: the lower-level rooms

In the west angle of the courtyard is a staircase leading to the series of lower-level roo
this series today extends without interruption along the full length of the main bu
ing whose façade looks out over the lake.

Whilst these buildings are often referred to as 'underground', they certainly do
deserve this title which seems to owe more to tradition than to fact. Their floor leve

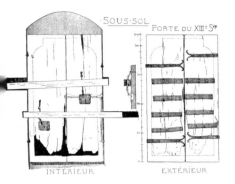

tually above the level of the lake. They date for the most part from the 13th century. With their ogival or barrel vaults and their columns, these rooms are clearly good exam- es of Gothic architecture. They were used as storerooms for weapons and merchan- se, as shelters for the garrison and as prisons.

e first two spaces (P.5 & Q.6) were both used as cellars and storehouses by the bailiff- stellans at the time of the Savoyards and then by the Bernese; it was always possible pass directly from the first to the second space. This second space also has two exits, e into the castle itself and the other giving onto the outside. The postern, hidden away the shadows, leads out onto the lake; just opposite is a staircase halfway up the wall, ich runs up inside the wall and comes out in the room above (Q.13); it was uncovered ring the 20th century and extended to reach the ground by means of a wooden stair- se which can still be seen. There were of course some practical advantages to this ease access, but it also offered the occupants of the castle the possibility, if need be, of caping without drawing too much attention to themselves. On the land side of the cas- the rock can be seen in places from here onwards, to a greater or lesser extent. This possible because the level of the floors was lowered about one century ago.

narrow and dark space (R.7) was originally separated from these two first rooms. It s now been opened up and after crossing it, one arrives in the first lower-level room the seigneur's part of the castle (S.8). This must have been the scene of tragic events. probably began life simply as a cellar, before being turned into a place of execution the 16th century. It is true that we do not know when the gallows was installed. Does ear witness to events in the distant past, or is it part of a scenography devised dur-

Postern (S), drawing of the medi-aeval door, published in 1923. *(Fondation du Château de Chillon. Photo Elise Heuberger)*

Friedrich Martens, Underground room in the Castle of Chillon, engraving published by the Bazar vaudois. A pilgrimage to Bonivard's column circa 1850. *(Zentralbibliothek Zurich, Graphis-che Sammlung)*

ing the 19th century to impress visitors? In this room is to be found the same system two exits as has already been seen before (Q.6). Here there is a large staircase whi gives access to the ground floor, and a postern, blocked by an iron grill. The postern w formerly hidden behind a heavy door in oak, reinforced with ironwork. The original do dating from the 13th century, was so decrepit that it was replaced by a copy in 19C today this copy is fixed to the wall. Two well-known episodes illustrate the decidedly d ferent ways in which these exits could be used. Guillaume Bolomier, the chancellor Savoy, was forced to leave the castle by this postern in 1446. Having fallen victim t political plot, he was condemned to death by drowning. The sentence was carried o from here and he died just off the rock on which the castle stands. In 1536, Antoine Beaufort was the commander of Chillon, the last remaining position occupied by t Savoyards. The Bernese army attacked, and Beaufort surrendered during the morni of March 29, stating that he would give up the castle during the afternoon. He ma use of these few hours to flee the castle, finding his way to freedom through the poste and then escaping by the lake. The vast room (U-U1-U2.9) next to this one will ever associated with the name of Bonivard, one of the prisoners whom the Bernese soldie found in the abandoned fortress. This majestic space, which had earlier been used a storeroom for goods and weapons, was converted into a prison as early as 1290. It w during the 19th century that it was to become famous, owing its notoriety to the p of Byron. Apart from the myth, however, it is certain that this space possesses a nu ber of features which are worthy of attention. Near the entry is a crucifixion scene s rounded by saints. This drawing in charcoal was executed during the mid 15th cent clearly by an experienced artist. It decorates one of the walls of what was formerl small closed room, known locally as a "crotton", namely a cell reserved, it was said,

Staircase (O) and its painted decoration.
(Fondation du Château de Chillon. Photo Elise Heuberger)

se who were condemned to death. The unexpected presence of this work of art in position has not yet been satisfactorily explained.

he other end of the room, an unusual technical detail can be seen. Shingles and small rds are trapped in the vault. These date from about 1250 and were components of frame set up for the construction of the vault. They were used to hold the mortar ween the blocks whilst it was drying. They must have been overlooked at the end he work, which can easily be understood since the room, given its intended purpose, s certainly not brightly lit.

castellan's courtyard (E)

buildings which were used by the Savoyard castellan and then, later, by the nese bailiff are arranged around the second courtyard (E.12); some of them can visited. A staircase (O), leading to the bailiff's residence, was constructed in 1643 he time of the bailiff Johann Stürler, who had his coat of arms (see also U1.18) ced on the door-head. This building still has its original white plasterwork in ces and also the painted decorations around the window frames and highlight- the quoins. This decoration, restored recently, allows us a glimpse of the cas- s appearance before its walls were stripped bare. The plaster was removed at the d of the 19th century during the archaeological campaigns, and the walls have ce been left as they were, without any covering; this permits the visitor, specialist ot, to see the building's history reflected in its structure. This decision, taken for cational reasons, also reflects the taste of the period, since a large number of dings of the late 19th century were constructed in stone which was left bare.

The castellan's room (Q) with its 15th-century ceiling supported on two oak columns circa 1270; view dating to circa 1890.
At the end of the room are the stove (1602) and the cupboard (1590) which is now in the *camera nova*.
(Fondation du Château de Chillon. Photo Elise Heuberger)

It does sometimes engender somewhat disconcerting effects, as can be seen on façade of the large neighbouring central building (Q) where heteroclite features juxtaposed.

This building, which was erected between 1260 and 1270, comprises two spac one above the other. On the ground floor, the constable's dining room (Q.13), a known as the "great Bernese kitchen", is a memory of an earlier division of t space. The partitions which separated the kitchen in the northern part of the ro from the antechamber and the salon in the southern sector were demolished as ea as 1836. The room as it is now bears a certain resemblance to the clerics' cham (G.31); some of the similarities are real, others have been imposed by the resto tion work carried out in the 20th century. It is lit by bays with double lancet windo and trefoil tracery, which are framed by a segmental arch. This form appeared Chillon for the first time shortly before 1265 in this very room. It is also here that chevron ornaments first made an appearance; in 1912-13, when the room v painted, this motif was reproduced on all of the walls. The wall-hangings, mad 1913, freely combine motifs taken from an altar-frontal woven after 1300 for Saint-Maurice Church, the actual Stadtkirche in Thun. The use of this design d not constitute an anachronism, since the piece originally here is believed to h dated from after 1300. They were – according to mediaeval ideas – intended to pieces which could be moved around, but they have in fact always remained in same place. However, the room is also remarkable for the quality of its mediae objects. In the centre of the room are two oak columns, each carved out of one pi of wood. Dating from circa 1270, they are one of the few surviving examples of t

28

e of support in Gothic architecture. They hold up the mid 15th-century ceiling, ated at the same time as the large fireplace. Two finely sculpted Renaissance rs, one of which has a pediment in which is to be found the coat of arms of the iff Von Mülinen, who commissioned the door in 1586, recall the redecoration k carried out during the Bernese period.

the upper storey, the room (Q.14), called *aula nova* in 1279, still deserves this ellation today. The space, which boasts a spectacular barrel-vaulted ceiling in d, was reconstructed in 1925-26, based on archaeological and documentary evi- ce. This type of ceiling is so rare that only one room with a similar structure — he castle of Grandson — is known. Chillon can be proud to have two such ceil- s, since a second one has also been reconstructed, on a more modest scale, in a jhbouring room (U.17).

room was not used during the Bernese period, and subsequently housed an arse- Later, during the 19th century, this room was used for cells for prisoners who thus the luxury of a view over the lake. After 1902, these cells became offices for the hitects working at the castle. The decision was taken during the 20th century to ore the room to its mediaeval state. Due to the tangled web of modifications, the m had undergone, this was based on rather tenuous reasoning, but the result ded to be imposing, given the ambitions for this room, which had been chosen to se the planned museum of Chillon and, more particularly, the collection of pons. Two possibilities were suggested for the reconstruction of the ceiling — flat aulted — and this shows the aesthetic character of the project. It was decided that

Aula nova (Q), 1902.
View looking towards Albert Naef's office, included in the Journal, f° 901g.
(ACV, N2. Photo Rémy Gindroz, Archéotech SA)

Aula nova (Q) looking towards the south.
(Fondation du Château de Chillon. Photo Elise Heuberger)

the ceiling should be vaulted; thus the visitor can today see this astonishing vau▌ wood, enhanced by the use of polychromy on the junction-plates, which freely i▌ tates certain fragments found in the castle. The walls, decorated with a cheque▌ pattern borrowed from the *camera domini* (X.19), also bear a large shield with the c▌ of arms of the House of Savoy, presumably dating from the 15th century.

The principal courtyard (F)

Around the **principal courtyard** (F.25) stands the residential complex of the Savoy fa▌ ily. Here are the staterooms (U1) with their adjoining secondary rooms (U & U2), the lo▌ ings (S, X & W), the chapel (Y) and the administrative buildings (G & K), protected▌ the donjon (I).

In the courtyard are two staircases leading to the *aula* and to the chapel, which se▌ to meet at the point where the crossed mullioned window of the *camera domini* i▌ be found. Fragments of the original decoration of this window, in red and blue, are ▌ visible. This architectural scenography drew attention to an important place in the c▌ tle, and it no doubt created a strong visual impact during the Middle Ages, since it st▌ out against the walls which, had a rather uniform appearance as they were covered v▌ plaster. The restorers decided at the beginning of the 20th century to remove the p▌ ter to reveal the underlying masonry. The rustic effect is heightened, but some of ▌ earlier majesty of this spot has been lost.

Only the first floor of the building at the end of the courtyard is open to the public; h▌ are to be seen the **antechamber** and the **Bernese bedroom** (S.15 & 16).

ll paintings decorate this room. These paintings are typically 17th century in terms both their style and their motifs. The other decorative elements are, however, no more in pastiche. The furniture was brought here in 1930, and recalls the Bernese period. e stone stove, bearing the date 1624, comes from Aigle, whilst the 17th-century tester has the coat of arms of the Schiner family, who came from the Valais. A small cor-or, which must have been cut into the south wall during the 13th century, certainly to the latrines projecting above the lake; these were reconstructed, along with the all adjoining gallery, in 1934.

he next room, the **guest room**, (U.17) the style of presentation chosen in 1920-22 ws the visitor to recognize the two major historical periods that have left their mark this room and its decoration. The lower parts of the walls have a grisaille decoration a white background, painted by Andreas Stoss in 1587-88; this was added after the m had been altered, and corresponds to the new dimensions. Above this is a painted oration with architectural motifs and a barrel-vaulted ceiling in wood: both of these tures clearly date from the Savoyard period. The room is divided by a low partition h a crenellated top, mediaeval in style. This is a reconstruction in plaster, based on ments excavated from the lower storey, and illustrates both a building technique and eans of dividing spaces and creating corridors, often used in the castle.

adjacent room, the **coat-of-arms hall** (U1.18), extends over the second storey of uilding constructed in the mid 13th century. Its bays dating from the 13th century, panelled ceiling and its 15th-century fireplace were all made while the castle nged to the Savoyards. During the Bernese period, this was the only large room in

Room of the coats of arms (U1) looking towards the south.
(Fondation du Château de Chillon. Photo Elise Heuberger)

the castle: its mediaeval splendour and spaces were maintained so that it could be u
for government. Hence, at the end of the 16th century, it was decorated with a rem
able series of wall paintings composed of ornamental designs in grisaille and, part
larly, a frieze of colourful coats of arms. This was to be added to over the course of
centuries, and constituted a record of the Bernese bailiffs who governed at Chillon.
is the most comprehensive set of coats of arms in mural form, which has been
served in the canton. Personal prestige is certainly manifested in this series, but
also a clear statement of the durability and the legitimacy of Bernese power in the a
power that was incarnated in the representatives of the most illustrious Bernese pa
cian families. These paintings were executed, in part at least, by a talented artist,
Bernese painter Andreas Stoss († 1619), whose career is closely associated with the
orative works commissioned for the major bailiff castles. The bailiff Hans Wilhelm
Mülinen invited Stoss in 1586, and drew up the scheme, which he was then to tra
late onto the south wall. His successors adopted the same tone, carrying on with
scheme until halfway along the wall giving onto the lake. This gave a homogen
appearance to the room. The series was brought to an abrupt halt just as work on
north wall was beginning, probably when the bailiffs moved to Vevey in 1733; it w
only be completed 1917-18. The coats of arms of the officials who held office from 1
to 1798 are presented here in two rows. A large shield with the coat of arms of V
accompanied by a commemorative inscription dated 1917, closes the series. Thus
allusion is made to the entrance gate, opposite, which bears the coat of arms of Be
and those of the man who had commissioned the paintings, with the date 1588.
From 1542 onwards, the *aula magna* (U1.26), on the lower storey, housed a mill
then a press, both of which were to be replaced by cannons during the 19th cent

32

vas the first room to be restored in the castle in 1899; it kept its ceiling and the h-century fireplace, alongside which are to be found benches dating from the 0s. These are replicas of late Gothic furniture found in the castle of Issogne (Val oste). This room also contains modern wall-hangings decorated with the arms of blais and of Savoy.

ding work on the Tower d'Allinges began during the 12th century. This part of the le owes its name to a powerful seigneurial family which possessed land on the thern banks of Lake Geneva, and whose links with Chillon are not entirely clear. The er contains two bedrooms. On the ground floor is to be found a room (X.27) whose t is marked by some troubled chapters, and which was restored in a pseudo-medi- al style during the 1930s. The various stages of this room's history are visible on its ls, in a somewhat crude archaeological staging; and as a result, this room can rcely hope to rival with the **camera domini** or seigneur's room (X.19) situated on next storey and which still reveals signs, albeit a little faded by the centuries, of ormer splendour. The room was made during the 13th century, and was then dered after 1336 by Count Aymon. A few years later, rich painted decoration was ed, created in 1341-44 by the official artist of the House of Savoy, Jean de Grand- who had collaborated with the Florentine painter Giorgio d'Aquila. Ever since the aeological work carried out at the beginning of the 20th century, this set of paint- shares the space with the remains of chequer pattern decoration dating from the of the 13th century, with some fragments of a decor in grisaille and some Bernese ts of arms painted by Stoss in 1587. After 1733, the room was converted into an nal and thereafter large shelves were placed on the north and west walls. In spite

North wall, area where the coats of arms from the beginning of the 18th century meet those painted by Ernest Correvon in 1917, on two rows.
The point where the two series meet is marked by part of the last 18th-century frame, prepared for the next bailiff. This is probably intentional.
(Fondation du Château de Chillon. Photo Elise Heuberger)

Johann Rudolf Rahn, the camera domini (X), drawing, 1886.
(Zentralbibliothek Zurich, Graphische Sammlung)

of these disfigurations, the room was already one of the important attractions dur
the 19th century, when the first tourists visited Chillon. Naef was particularly fon
the room and a careful examination of it was made between 1905 and 1914. Rest
tion work was done on it at this time, and further work was carried out in 1946-50 a
then in 1978-82.

Above wall-hangings and a frieze of coats of arms are to be seen both real and im
nary animals, who move about in an enclosed, idealized realm. Fleurs de lys agai
a blue background and Savoy crosses on a red background cover the ceiling. The te
nique used was unusual, since these motifs were made of sheets of pewter glue
the ceiling. The fleurs de lys were varnished to imitate gilding. The pieces have si
fallen off, so that today the motifs are seen in negative. When it was first created
candlelight this ceiling must have scintillated like a starry sky.

This painted ensemble may well appear to be simple, but concealed within it are s
eral levels of interpretation, typical of the taste for this type of learned prestidigita
which developed during the 14th century. The omnipresent heraldic decorations
intended to emphasize the lineage. The interpretation of the strew-pattern needs t
approached with more nuance. The cross, a Christian symbol and a common hera
device, must refer to the Savoy dynasty. For historical reasons the fleur de lys does
here refer only to French royalty; it is also to be read as an attribute of the Virgin.
selection and the arrangement of the other elements depend on symbolical and to
graphical criteria. Thus the animals — generally kept in princely menageries becaus
their status as curiosities and as signs of wealth — are cleverly arranged across the sp

Torture chamber (U2).
*(Fondation du Château de Chillon.
Photo Elise Heuberger)*

cely any iconographical and stylistic equivalent can be found for this ensemble, rich
eaning and sophisticated in its execution.

two rooms nearby, one above the other, were used as a retreat. On the upper floor
e **drawing room** (U2.20); under the plasterwork on one of the walls here the irreg-
ty of the underlying masonry can be clearly seen. This is in fact one of the walls,
nally an external wall, of the Tour d'Allinges, and it demonstrates the considerable
of this part of the building. At the level of the courtyard is a room (U2.28) which was
ibly used from the mid 17th century onwards as an interrogation chamber. It is for
reason that it is now known as the **torture room**, and its use as such during the
century is confirmed. The colours and the pleasant appearance of the room seem
elie its rather sombre title. However, it was in fact only at the end of the 19th cen-
that the coats of whitewash were removed from these walls, revealing the poly-
my which was then restored and touched up in places. The painted motifs between
panels on the ceiling were borrowed in 1898 from a wall painting to be found in a
se in eastern Switzerland.

two-storey building housing the **latrines** (V.21 & 29) was constructed in the mid 13th
cury on a part of the site which had no doubt long been used for this purpose. Naef
gests that there were latrines, called bartizan latrines, projecting from the walls of
two adjoining buildings (U2 & X), before the construction of the building that is there
. The waste was carried into the lake by ducts running inside the wall, which emp-
out onto a large sloping surface underneath an arch. This type of construction, used
dumping ground, could also at times be employed for defensive purposes. To ensure

the greatest comfort for the castle's inhabitants, these latrines were usually located n
the residential areas. A reconstruction of such bartizan latrines, popular since the 1
century, can be seen at Chillon (S.16).

The main building (W), adjoining the Tower d'Allinges, was, built towards 1375 on
orders of Amédée VI, thought Naef. The two rooms in the building were reserved
Amédées's wife, Countess Bonne de Bourbon who stayed at Chillon for a leng
period in 1379. On the upper floor (W.22), only the three crossed mullioned windo
looking out over the lake, belong to the castle. The 15th-century ceiling comes fro
private house in Villeneuve whilst the wood panels were created after originals for
in the same house and were installed at Chillon around 1930.

The lower room, called the *camera nova* (W.30), was restored in 1930 so that
Association's committee meetings could take place there. It contains two rem.
able objects. The stove was purchased in 1888; decorated with the coat of a
of Lutry and bearing the date 1602, this stove was made for the former town
in Lutry. Its lower part is in stone; above which rises a tower covered with tiles m
by the potter Henri Baud from Fribourg. This is the oldest complete stove to h
survived in the canton of Vaud and it is the earliest well-documented exampl
the corpus of Fribourg stoves. Opposite this is to be found a splendid walnut c
board. Its apparent sobriety masks the great skill displayed in its execution.
impressively large piece of furniture, which arrived at the castle in 1590, co
from the house of lieutenant bailiff Ferdinand Bouvier at Villeneuve and is on
the few remaining objects attesting to the original furnishings of the castle.

**Albert Naef in the courtyard (G)
before the reconstruction of the
lower room, 1893.**
(ACV, N2. Photo Rémy Gindroz,
Archéotech SA)

northernmost side of the castle is today a courtyard (G). This area used to con-
the upper floor of an administrative building constructed between 1261 and
6, called the *domus clericorum*, that is the clerics' house. Each storey was given
r to one room such as, here, the *pelium* (G.23); the word stove was also used in
ther vague way to refer to a heated room. Many archaeological remains prove
there was a tiled stove in this room around 1350. At some stage during the 16th
tury, either before or after the arrival of the Bernese, the interior structure of this
ding disappeared, either because it collapsed or because it was demolished:
ion is divided as to the exact details and date of this structural change. The
ce was organized for defensive purposes, possibly after 1536, when the wooden
ered way was added. Further work to improve the defences was carried out
ards the end of the 17th century, including the addition of the watchtower. When
lower room was reconstructed, the former *pelium* was returned to its original
l and remained a courtyard. Below is to be found the **clerics' chamber** (G.31);
cessive stages of work in this room have allowed it to regain its original medi-
al appearance. The joisted ceiling, made by enlarging an original ceiling which
ier covered a neighbouring space (U2.28), dates from 1938. The wall decorations
e done in the 1950s to fit the room; the model used here was traces of medi-
al paintings which had survived on the internal wall of the earlier building,
pite lengthy exposure to the elements.

the upper floor of a building used for defensive purposes and constructed
ween the two enclosures is the **chapel of Saint Georges** (Y.24). This was a place
evotion reserved exclusively for the Counts and then the Dukes of Savoy; and from

time to time it was used to safeguard treasures. Built at the beginning of the 13
century, the chapel is lit by bays dating from circa 1250; one of these – in the chev
– was then walled up in 1260, when a further storey was added to the adjoini
tower (Z). The vault was added at the end of the 13th century; a master Jacques a
two assistants executed the painted decoration in 1314. Since 1336, direct acce
to the *camera domini* is possible thanks to a spiral staircase. The chapel was aba
doned at the time of the Reformation, and was subsequently used as a loft, powc
magazine and arsenal, before becoming a chapel again in 1856. Coats of whitewa
were removed in 1908, and the paintings underneath were restored and retouch
in 1914-16. Between 1985 and 1995, a new series of examinations of and work
the paintings was begun but was never completed. The door and the steel floor c
ering, indicating the position of the former altar, also dated from this time.

The paintings, whose style shows traces of Italian and English influences, we
planned as an ensemble for Amédée V, a demanding and cultivated patron. The ma
subject is Christ, and the themes chosen illustrate his genealogy, his life on ea
and his resurrection. The themes are organized very carefully in the space availab
On the vaults, there are figures from the Old Testament and also Saint John the Ba
tist. The northern and southern walls show figures from the New Testament,
Evangelists and apostles. The two other walls are in such a bad state of repair t
any attempt to interpret the paintings is doomed to remain mere conjecture. M
est in size, on a rectangular plan and with a chevet lit by three bays, this is the ty
of castle chapel that the Savoyards favoured in the mid 13th century, characteria
as it is by Cistercian severity. Private chapels like this one were often included in

stles built in this region by the House of Savoy and their vassals. At the time of
e Reformation, they were generally destroyed or vandalized; Chillon is the excep-
n to the rule. On the lower storey, the room (Y.32) dating from the end of the 12th
ntury may also have housed a chapel; this would seem to be suggested by the
usual horizontal bays and the vault. However, by the mid 13th century, this had
en abandoned and the room was thereafter used as a storeroom.

e **treasury building** (K.41), found in a protected area of the castle, is known to
ve existed since at least 1287-88. It was built specifically for guarding currency,
ecious objects and archives. To reinforce the security only the vaulted room on the
per floor, a sort of office, could be reached from the *camera domini*, via the cov-
ed way. It was used as a prison from the mid 16th century and in 1815 it was
cided that the building should be used merely to house the staircase leading to
e donjon.

e keep or the **donjon** (I.42-46), built in three stages, rises from the centre of the rock.
s large Romanesque tower, on a quadrangular plan, doubtless dates from the 11th
ntury; according to Naef, upper storeys were added in the mid 13th century, and it
s then crowned with battlements. A further storey, with covered crenelles was
ded in 1304-05, bringing the tower to its height of 26 meters – about 85 feet (with-
: the roof). The tower as it is today is the result of work carried out from 1900 to 1910.
ce then, the walls reveal traces of the various construction phases, such as the top
the earliest tower, estimated to have been 15-16m (about 52 ft) high, and the
lled-in crenelles from the second building stage. Inside the tower, the floor levels

North façade of the donjon (I)
before the work, late 19th century.
*(Fondation du Château de Chillon.
Photo Elise Heuberger)*

Donjon (I) at the entrance level.
*(Fondation du Château de Chillon.
Photo Elise Heuberger)*

The building (H) is opened up during the excavations in the courtyard, 1900. Otto Schmid talking with Albert Naef, who is on the footbridge.
(ACV, N2. Photo Rémy Gindroz, Archéotech SA)

d the staircases have in part been reconstructed, using material from the old
ors which were in the large rooms on the side overlooking the lake.

e early entrance door opens, characteristically, 8m (26 ft) above the ground in the
uthern façade. Access to it was had by means of a ladder or a drawbridge. One of
se has been reconstructed, after a model known from the castle at Yverdon-les-Bains;
 to be found against the west face of the donjon, leading to a later entrance. Dur-
 the Middle Ages, and also during later periods, the donjon had a number of func-
ns. Nor should it be forgotten that this type of construction also had a considerable
nbolic force as a grandiloquent expression of power. It provided the last refuge in times
siege, but it was also an observation post, a warehouse and a prison – in the lower,
 it areas of the building. The only part of the building that was habitable is at the
rance level, a space which has two cupboards placed against the western wall. Nev-
neless, given that there is no fireplace here and that there are few windows, it seems
kely that it was used for living quarters except in extreme circumstances. Seen from
 point of view of its military purposes, it is an example of a time-honoured defence
tic. Any assailant who hazarded the treacherous path leading towards the final hid-
-place of his enemy was obliged to reveal his right flank to the defenders, which was
re vulnerable because unprotected by his shield.

curtain courtyard (H)

 visit begins in the basement of a **main building** (H.33), situated between the
 enclosures and connecting to the room of the models (Y.32). Three arrow-slits,
ntical to those to be found in the lower regions of the outer enclosure or curtain
1 & L.36), light this former storeroom, which was used for defensive purposes

and constructed circa 1200. These openings, the oldest in the castle, are of a type wh appeared early – circa 1180 – in France and England. The room was filled in after collapse of its vaults in the 15th century, and was forgotten about until the beginn of the 20th century, when it was rebuilt after the discovery of materials left in this a proved the former existence of construction here.

The upper part of the building, possibly a simple loggia placed against the south wall of the chapel, formerly concealed the northern part of the courtyard (H.34) has disappeared, and was probably demolished by the Bernese, who wished enlarge this courtyard, the only truly horizontal one to be found in the castle. Sir that time, this open space has taken on a new appearance. Part of it is filled v the glacis, the large block of rock with a facing, which was removed in 1902. It da from the first building activity on the rock and was no doubt reinforced during 12th century.

Situated in the centre of the defensive zone of the castle, this area allows us to unc stand the different structural elements – enclosures and towers – and the various m ifications which they underwent, be this for reason of military requirements or the ne to adapt the building for the use of firearms. However, it is only possible to appreci the lower parts of the curtain and of the towers from the other side of the moat, a leaving the fortress.

The 11th-century **inner enclosure** was reinforced and a crenellated battlement v added at the end of the 12th or the beginning of the 13th century; this work was d

42

at the outer enclosure could be better watched. The crenelles, which are still vis-
n the wall, were raised but then filled in during the 15th century, so that key-shaped
noles and small rectangular openings could be inserted. The **outer enclosure**, which
ne dated thanks to its low arrow-slits, was constructed at the end of the 12th cen-
It was raised in parts during the 13th century, and this work was then extended
entire length after 1536; at which time two rows of key-shaped loopholes were
ed, which can still be seen from the level of the courtyard.

here, all that can be seen of the **three semicircular towers** protecting the enclo-
are their outlines, the result of building work during the 14th and 15th centuries.
first tower (Z), adjoining the chapel cannot be visited; access to the others (Z1.35
37) is via the wooden covered way dating from the Bernese period.

in 1230, the towers reinforced the enclosure. This was thus only a short time
r the foundation of Villeneuve and its tollhouse, which constituted a new
e of operations on the major commercial route of the Great Saint Bernard, to
ch the Savoyards were keen to give privilege. Their plan is rectangular on the
rior side of the wall, developing into a semicircle on the outside of the wall. This
n unusual plan, seldom seen in castle architecture and the towers represented
nsiderable innovation in terms of defensive structures usually seen in the sur-
nding area. They have arrow-slits which are still Romanesque in style and
ch are never placed one above the other, in order to ensure the solidity of the
cture and to increase the range covered when shooting.

The curtain courtyard (H) looking
toward the glacis.
*(Fondation du Château de Chillon.
Photo Elise Heuberger)*

South and eastern sides.
*(Fondation du Château de Chillon.
Photo Elise Heuberger)*

Tower (C), at the level of the earlier small rooms.
(Fondation du Château de Chillon. Photo Elise Heuberger)

Tower (Z), showing the three storeys added in successive building phases.
(Fondation du Château de Chillon. Photo Elise Heuberger)

Later adaptations were a result of certain military requirements and also of a g
eral climate of insecurity. Further height was added to the towers between 1260
1265 and they were topped with covered crenelles. At this time wooden galle
were also added; some of the supports for these were reconstructed during the 2
century to illustrate their position and can be seen on the side of the wall overl
ing the moat. In 1377-79, the towers were given a new masonry structure, which
new in the area, namely machicolations. Their supports were levelled down, but
still be seen under the new machicolations added during the 15th century. At the l
of the 1260 covered crenelles which can be visited, it was decided to create roc
with panelled ceilings and fireplaces. This type of belvedere, a place for quiet refl
tion or solitary study, was becoming increasingly common in princely lodgings c
ing the period. These rooms, certainly in keeping with the taste of the times, w
one of the alterations made in view of Bonne de Bourbon's sojourn at the castl
1379. Then problems relating to the structure entailed new construction w
Toward 1450, Aymonet Corniaux had to demolish the earlier machicolations, wh
brackets were disintegrating. Above this, he erected the uppermost structure
machicolations and covered crenelles, which still exists today. The windows w
closed by bascule siege shutters; those which can be seen today were reconstruc
recently based on the evidence from a fragment found in the moat. The up
storeys of the towers were used for defensive purposes for a long time, whereas
lower storeys were sometimes used to house prisoners. The final modification ma
to the castle's defensive structures during the 17th century, came in the form of r
tangular bays which were cut into the walls and the curtain in various places.

he southernmost part of the courtyard, there is a covered area (L.36), an old large
eption room in the shape of a gallery, the *logia magna parlamenti*. It was here that
Savoyard princes and their castellans held audiences and dispensed justice. From
5 to 1536, it housed the castellan's kitchen, according to Naef. At the time of the
nese domination, it was partially demolished so that it could be converted into a com-
nd post overlooking the first courtyard (D), from where our visit started.

se then are the spaces which the public can visit in the Castle of Chillon, one of the
st famous fortresses in Europe. It inspires admiration because of its military instal-
ons, the harmonious arrangement of the parts of the building, the famous figures who
e stayed there and the beauty of its setting. Not to mention, of course, the archae-
gical and historical secrets which Chillon keeps for itself and which it will perhaps
er be persuaded to divulge.

Logia magna parlamenti (L).
*(Fondation du Château de Chillon.
Photo Elise Heuberger)*

GLOSSARY

Arrow-slit: vertical slit pierced into a wall for shooting arrows and, here, according the ancient inventories of the castle, especially for shooting with crossbows which w more powerful.

Bailiff: officer who represents the prince in judiciary, administrative, fiscal and milit matters, at the head of the bailiwick.

Bailliage: a region defined in administrative and judiciary terms, under the respor bility of a bailiff and reuniting several castellanies.

Bartizan: a small over-hanging construction, often for defensive purposes, contain a small room, generally projecting from an angle at the top of a tower.

Castellan: administrator appointed by the Count of Savoy to administrate the cast lany; dismissible, often a member of the minor local nobility or foreign noble.

Castellany: subdivision of the bailiwick, administrative, judiciary and military u grouping several villages around a castle.

Course: a continuous horizontal layer of stones or bricks in a wall.

Covered crenelles: defensive crenelles at the top of a tower or an enclosure, cove with a horizontal piece of wood or stone, thus forming a window.

Crossed mullioned window: window divided into lights by vertical bars (mullions) a horizontal bars (transoms).

Curtain: in military architecture, an enclosure situated between two tours.

Glacis: term used since Naef which designates a facing put onto the rock, on the la ward side, at the foot of the two enclosure walls.

hole-shaped: refers to the shape of a type of loophole.

cet: tall narrow window topped with a pointed arch.

phole: slit pierced in a wall to allow firing of weapons, particularly suitable for rms.

chicolation: construction in stone similar to the wooden gallery: it had the same tions, was of the same form and was positioned similarly.

at: ditch filled with water which protected the walls and the towers of a castle.

tern: door hidden in an external wall.

mental arch: arch whose segment is lower than a semicircle.

ery: ornamental intersecting stonework subdividing a bay.

oil: decorated with three lobes or leaf-shaped curves.

den gallery: structure in wood projecting from the top of towers or enclosures, with s in its floor through which projectiles could be dropped to the bottom of the wall w.

ABBREVIATIONS AND BIBLIOGRAPHY

ACV: Archives cantonales vaudoises.
CAR: Cahiers d'archéologie romande.
JOURNAL: Journal : Château de Chillon. Journal des travaux, des fouilles, trouvai accidentelles, incidents, etc. et de l'exploration archéologique du château.
MCAH: Musée cantonal d'archéologie et d'histoire, Lausanne.
SHSR: Société d'histoire de la Suisse romande.

Selected recent titles which include a good survey of numerous publications the castle, including Naef's works.

— Andenmatten Bernard, *La Maison de Savoie et la noblesse vaudoise (XIIIᵉ-XIVᵉ s.): sup orité féodale et autorité princière,* Lausanne, 2005 (Mémoires et Documents de SHSR, 4/VIII).

— Bertholet Denis, Huguenin Claire, Feihl Olivier (dir.), *Autour de Chillon. Archéologie restauration au début du siècle,* Lausanne, 1998 (Document du MCAH).

— Chausson Jacques-David, *Mémorial de l'Association pour la restauration du châte de Chillon,* Veytaux, 1987.

— Raemy Daniel de, (dir.), *Chillon. La chapelle,* Lausanne, 1999 (CAR, 79).

— Raemy Daniel de, *Châteaux, donjons et grandes tours dans les états de Savoie (12 1330). Un modèle: le château d'Yverdon,* Lausanne, 2004 (CAR, 98 et 99).